T0153247

TIGER FUR

TIGER FUR

BY SALGADO MARANHÃO

Translated by Alexis Levitin

WHITE PINE PRESS / BUFFALO, NEW YORK

WHITE PINE PRESS
P.O. Box 236 Buffalo, New York 14201
www.whitepine.org

A Pelagem da Tigra copyright © 2009 by Salgado Maranhão
English translation copyright © 2015 by Alexis Levitin

All rights reserved. This work, or portions thereof, may not be reproduced
in any form without the written permission of the publisher.

Acknowledgments:

First, I must thank Salgado Maranhão, who, in his small apartment in Urca, worked
with me indefatigably and with great good humor until the task was done. Next, I would
like to thank, once again, Prof. Luiz Fernando Valente of Brown University, whose
faith in both of us led to our happy collaboration. Thanks, as well, to SUNY-Platts-
burgh for supporting my travel to Rio de Janeiro to work on this book. Thanks also to
the Plattsburgh State Art Museum for the watercolor "Tiger" by James Fitzgerald that
graces our cover. Also, thanks to Fernando Beleza for his help with the two difficult
sonnets. And great thanks to my old friend Ann Tracy, who accepts my late night lin-
guistic phone queries with unflappable good will and unflagging intellectual energy.

I would also like to acknowledge prior publication of all of these translations, some-
times in slightly different versions, in the following literary magazines: *Artful Dodge*,
The Bitter Oleander, *Brasil/Brazil*, *Ezra*, *Loch Raven Review*, *Moon City Review*, *Natural
Bridge*, *Osiris*, *Per Contra*, *Sirena*, *Spoon River Poetry Review*, *Springhouse Journal*.

Obra publicada com o apoio do
Ministério da Cultura do Brasil / Fundação Biblioteca Nacional.

MINISTÉRIO DA CULTURA
Fundação BIBLIOTECA NACIONAL

Publication of this book was made possible, in part, by support from the Ministry of
Culture of Brazil / National Library Foundation, the National Endowment for the
Arts, which believes that a great nation deserves great art, and with public funds from
the New York State Council on the Arts, a State Agency.

ART WORKS.
arts.gov

State of the Arts

NYSCA

Cover art: "Tiger" by James Fitzgerald with permission of the Plattsburgh State Art
Museum

First Edition

ISBN: 978-1-935210-71-9

Printed and bound in the United States of America.
Library of Congress Control Number: 2014960006

Contents

Translator's Preface

In a writer's manifesto from 2009, Salgado Maranhão and his collaborator Geraldo Carneiro wrote: "Poetry is not just a question of truth, but of ecstasy. That's why we are poets of ecstasy: the ecstasy of language, the ecstasy of life."

In this volume, ecstasy and anguish are, as in life itself, commingled. This is a book about love and the heights to which it lifts us and the depths to which it flings us down. It is a book about the extremity of our emotional possibilities. It is also about the extremes to which language can be wrought.

Salgado and I both believe that the art of poetry is highly musical. This shared belief informs our collaborative effort. For us, the major challenge, beyond the lexical, is to discover how the original created its emotional and spiritual effects through language, through sound, and to see how the English translation can arrive at a similar result through its own tonalities, its own music.

Both of us have linguistic limitations that we struggle, together, to overcome. For example, Salgado has minimal English. However, he is extremely musical. The title of his newest book, launched in June 2015, suggests as much: *Opera of Nos.* In addition to his ten books of poetry, he has written song lyrics and made recordings with some of Brazil's leading jazz and pop musicians. As we have worked together these past six or seven years, we have gotten into a routine that goes far beyond questions of lexical fidelity. We have agreed that the most profound fidelity to the original is in the music of the language. And that involves not just consonants and vowels, but questions of velocity, abruptness, gentleness, acuteness, agility, humor, and playfulness, as part of the movement of language. And that fidelity, paradoxically, must extend in both directions: toward the original, the source, and toward the new, the target tongue.

Our collaboration always involves rereading aloud both the original and the translation. We listen to each other's words, to the music of the two versions of the text. Often, Salgado will explain why he has chosen a specific word. Often he will remind me of his affection for polysemy, the fertile possibilities within a word that allow it to spread suggestively in different directions, towards different meanings. Whenever we encounter one of his neologisms, he explains the elements from which it is built. Whenever I come up with a solution he listens attentively. If he likes the sound, he often will favor that aspect of the translation, and allow much leeway in the lexical sphere. In the end, it is our shared faith in the essential contribution of music to the "meaning" of a poem that enables us to work together as true brothers in arms.

Some small examples of my practice. In "Pré-Logos II," the poem's rather violent conclusion depicts, I assume, the child-god Eros (though represented by an amalgam of the Portuguese word for God and the Yoruba word for the intermediary between the God Orisha and you.) The final image in the original is: ó raio/que se desgarra/a sujar de luz a vida." In terms of sound, the emotion is supported in the original principally by the echoes between "se desgarra and sujar." In English, however, I was able to support the poet's feeling of betrayal and disgust through interwoven patterns of alliteration, consonance, and assonance, heightened by a spondaic insistence:

> oh lightning
> bolt burst free
> to make life filthy with your light.

We have both alliteration and assonance in "lightning/life/light," supported by the quieter consonantal echoes in "bolt" and "filth." We also have the obvious alliterative pair of "bolt burst." For me, this texture of interrelated sounds conveys the poet's feelings perhaps more persuasively even than the original.

Despite, or because of, the intensity of passion depicted in this work, Salgado imposes apparently domesticating patterns on a number of the later poems. "Nadirs," for example, is a fully rhymed sonnet. It took me months to wrestle the translation into submission and some readers would argue it was not worth the effort, because it caused me to stray too far from the original's meaning. For example, the witch-like "bubbling yeast" is indeed my own invention, to allow for a rhyme with "beast." But I reported all my strayings to Salgado and read the English aloud and he was so pleased with the harmony of the rhymed sonnet in English, that the lexical deviations seemed relatively unimportant. For me, the strictures of the formal pattern cannot be ignored, because without them the poem is no longer passion beating against the shackles of a long-established form. But many of my friends and fellow translators disagree, preferring to keep the freedom of unrhymed diction, with which they feel they can better approximate the lexical and even metaphoric truths of the original. There is never just one path.

In the last poem of this collection, the poem that gives the book its name, Salgado contemplates the illusory nature of the fire of Eros. The woman who provoked his own madness is either the metaphoric tiger of this book or else its cunning mistress. Let us look at some of the imagery and rhymes that hold this final sonnet together. The original contemplates the nature of impassioned fibers of fire in these terms:

> Perhaps they're made of a tiger's coat
> (that might be hiding a volcano in its lava)
> pretending that it's staying when in fact it's leaving
> pretending it is kissing when really it is sinking in its fangs.

My intermediary stage was both accurate and shockingly unpoetic. But here is what the imperative of form drove or lured me to:

> Or maybe they are made of tiger's fur
> (that hides volcanic flames behind its play)
> to sink its fangs as it pretends to purr,
> to go away as it pretends to stay.

The play and the purring are both invented, and both suggest the endearing qualities of a charming little tiger, not yet unleashed. Of course we see that the purr is pretend while the tiger fur (with its volcanic flames) is real. And we see that both the kittenish play and the feigned staying are pretense.

These two sonnets were, quite naturally, the last poems in the book to be finished. I was unable to complete them in Brazil, despite the desire Salgado and I shared to finish our translation collaboration together. Only far away, after the passage of several months, was I able to find the license to approach my own literal translations and begin to transform them into functioning sonnets in English. It may seem as if distance allowed irreverence to seep in. And from the point of view of strict lexical fidelity, that is true. But what replaced reverence for the lexical truth of the original sonnet was a reverence for the flesh and freshness of the new sonnet, nurtured by the new language.

In the end, I feel the translator, strangely enough, must have a divided allegiance, a divided fidelity. He must be faithful in two directions: to the spirit of the original and to the spirit of his own tongue, from which he draws forth something new, a homage. For all of you, here is the English side by side with the Portuguese. For those of you who speak both languages, you may enjoy reimagining the formal poems in your own way. But I do hope that in striving to be true to my native tongue I have not strayed so far from the original truth in Portuguese as to seem a traitor. *Traduttore, traditore.* Can we ever be true?

Alexis Levitin – Plattsburgh, New York
June, 2015

A PELAGEM DA TIGRA   /   TIGER FUR

Pré-logos I

O amor editou suas garras
em meu delírio:
                        móbile/
                                    meteoro
a blefar
seu fogo rasante.

De algum rugir indomável
(submerso como o pulsar
das pedras) sinto

o vórtice
do seu brilho
                na jugular.

Por isso grito
para que as palavras
me reconheçam.

Assombros, raios, névoa,
alastram-me
esta ambígua paisagem
dos olhos.

Tudo que rege
a grafia sísmica presente
no que dista
ou impalpável
como o esquecimento.

Pre-Logos I

Love left its claws engraved
in my delirium:
                      mobile/
                          meteor
deluding
with its furtive flame.

From some indomitable roar
(submerged like the pulsing
within stones) I feel

the vortex
of its gleaming
                    in my jugular.

That's why I scream
so the words
will know me.

Terror, lightning, fog
spread
an ambiguous landscape
before my eyes.

All that governs
seismic signs present still
in what grows distant
or untouchable
like forgetting.

Pré-logos II

Trata-se de fogo
indiferente
       à combustão: caldeira
que se nutre
do que percute.

Um carpir rente ao nada,
um certo aqui/
alhures.

Ante o silêncio
        que espreita
e a febre
que desacata os limites,
um reino se declara.

E o que busca
esse deus-erê
ao revés do que exorta, ó raio
que se desgarra
a sujar de luz a vida?

Pre-Logos II

It's a question of a fire
indifferent
         to combustion: a furnace
feeding on
the thing that beats.

A weeping on the edge of nothingness,
a certain here
somewhere else.

Before the silence
               that observes
and the fever that affronts all limits,
a kingdom now declares itself.

And what is that child-god
looking for
contrary to its exhortations, oh lightning
bolt burst free
to make life filthy with your light?

MAR DE LAVAS

"Lenta salix quantum pallenti cedit oliuae."

Virgílio

SEA OF FLAMES

"Lenta salix quantum pallenti cedit olivae."

Vergil

1.

Ante a espessura
                    do teu brilho
e o esquivo sopro
das palavras
                    há um rito
que pede para amanhecer.

Tão íntimo como o interlúdio
tece a sua lenda

ou o flagrante (flerte!)
em que a pupila
coagula o gesto.

Raiam para dentro
da noite nômade a
discreta mudez do mergulho
e as lavas do coração
deserto.

Caminho longamente
sobre o guizo das pedras
e das sílabas.

1.

Before the density
                of your blaze
and the elusive breath
of words,
          there is a rite
begging for its dawn.

As intimate as an interlude
it weaves its legend

or the flagrant moment (the flirtatious look!)
in which the pupil
coagulates the gesture, the gestation.

The discreet silence of the plunge
and the lava of the empty
heart
send piercing rays into
the nomad night.

On and on I go
along the rattling of the stones
and syllables.

2.

Quando amanheço
e te oferto o dia
em fatias (no lapso
em que o traço
é voz e nem o vivido
importa, mas o impresso),

longe do que me afere,
o dar-me despe
sua dimensão de casca
e pérola.

Algo que, sutil, lateja
como se dos ossos
brotassem pétalas.

Entram na composição
do gesto:
    a) as pequenas rachaduras da alma;
    b) as infiltrações da espera;
    c) as prestações do amor em atraso.

Daí a dor de concreto,
daí a dor sem alarde,
que dói no sonho,
não na carne.

2.

When I dawn
and offer you the day
in slices (in the instant
when line or sign
is voice and what is lived
of no importance, just what is engraved),

far from evaluations,
my surrender strips away
the world of shell
and pearl.

Something that, subtle, pulses
as if petals were blossoming
from bones.

Joining the formulation
of the gesture:
    a) the little fissures of the soul;
    b) the seeping away of hope;
    c) overdue installments of love.

And thus the pain of the concrete,
and thus a pain without pretense,
that aches in dreams,
not in the flesh.

3.

Na esteira do que é silente
ou súplice
            zine
o furtivo sol das vozes

(inda
que seja apenas
um terçar de nervos
a rondar o verso
como libélulas de fogo), ali
um halo de música
sulca
        o desejo. E
uma fome secreta
acorda cicatrizes.

E há de ser sempre
esse *game*/gumes,
essa dúbia dádiva
entre o que envulva
e o que envala?

3.

In the wake of what is silent
or supplicant
the furtive sun of voices
                    shrills.

(May there still be
just
the clash of nerves
prowling round the verse
like dragonflies of fire), and there
a halo of music
furrowing deep
                    desire. And
a secret hunger
awakens scars.

And will there always be
that etching/edge,
that grifter's gift
between what enters womb
and tomb?

4.

Transidos os versos tocam
tua carne
como se buscassem
um elo de música.

(Ó tesouro de lábios!)

Como se o silêncio
                    exilado
erguesse
uma réstia de júbilo.

Transido (em rubracor)
o coração clama
ciclamens sob a voragem
do mar
sem porto. Chove

no sangue e na trama
e chove onde a palavra enlaça
o olho tísico da ausência.

4.

Possessed the verses touch
your flesh
as if in search
of a link to music.

(Oh the treasure of the lips!)

As if silence
                exiled
were holding up
a vestige of exaltation.

Possessed (in rubyred)
the heart cries
for cyclamens beneath the churning
of a sea
without a port. It rains

in the blood and in the plot
and it rains where the word embraces
the haggard eye of absence.

5.

É como se a noite (lésbica) lambesse
- em meus olhos -
a tua aresta. E o lábio
sangrasse não no beijo,
mas no indício.
                    É desse frêmito
que as veias
ganem, desse espectro
de lúmen (a clamar
no telúrico
e no espermágico), quando

te olho
da fenda aberta
no interior das palavras.

Miríades de tempo súplice
sobre a voragem do mar
sem lume.

É desse rasgo
que os sonhos gritam,
dessa ambígua certeza.

5.

It's as if the (Lesbian) night were licking
—in my eyes—
your contoured flesh. And the lip
were bleeding not from a kiss,
but from a hint.
                            It is from this tremor
that the veins
whimper, from this ghostly
shimmer (clamoring
in telluric
and spermagic realms), when

I see you
through the fissure opening
in the interior of words.

Myriads of time suppliant
above the raging of a sea
without light.

It is from that tear
that dreams cry out,
from that ambiguous certainty.

6.

Perdi o abrigo
dos espelhos. Perdi
o álibi
        e a vertigem
que amanhece os olhos.

Fundido à minha
carnadura
o coração inunda
transparências.

Na casa do amor
urtigas habitam símbolos. E
o sangue
tingiu a manhã
sobre o teu nome.

Agora, lavra
lâmina iridecente, larva-me!
Na fita onde o grito rasga
a escrita.

Namoro uma lenda
numa cidade sem voz

e sobrevivo de abismos.

6.

I've lost the protection
of mirrors. I've lost
the alibi
        and the giddiness
that makes the eyes grow light.

Fused to my
body's flesh
the heart overflows
its transparencies.

In the house of love
nettles dwell in symbols. And
blood
has dyed morning
over your name.

Now, thrust home
the iridescent blade, truss me!
On the tape where a scream rips
through the script.

I love a legend
in a city without a voice

and I've survived the abyss.

7.

Por vezes o que reluta
é o que transmuta: pétalas

de água lambendo a pedra.

Febris os lábios rompem
o acorde que a voz simula.

E tua ausência
é o que delata esta argila
que sangra. E há outro

alarme a terçar
onde as palavras
     enlouquecem:

esta seita que exorta
ao canto e ao gesto
estendido ao mar.

Mesmo quando a rota
é só um nome,
mesmo quando o desabrigo
é colo.

7.

Sometimes what refutes
transmutes: petals

of water licking stone.

Lips, fevered, break
the chord the voice pretends to.

It is your absence
that strips bare this clay
that bleeds. And there's another

alarm battling
where words
              are driven mad:

this cult that exhorts
to song and to a gesture
spread across the sea.

Even when the route
is just a name,
even when forlornness
is a lap.

8.

Símiles do que a voz
enlaça ao deserto, são
teus ritos ínvios, símiles

do vôo
        sem rota.

Recolho-me à música
que o amor secreta
em teu gesto:
                cítaras
que ouço guizos.

E penso
na paisagem corroída
em que o silêncio
constrói sua pronúncia;

penso nas linhas
em que se afogam destinos (siglas
cambiantes
            do desejo) e vórtices
no olho do furacão.

8.

Similes with which the voice
entwines the desert,
your shifting rituals, similes

of flight
            without a plan.

I take refuge in the music
love secretes
through all your gestures:
                              zithers
that I hear as rattles.

And I think
of the eroded landscape
in which silence
constructs its pronouncement;

I think of the lines
in which destinies drown (wandering
brand names
            of desire), whirlwinds
in the eye of the storm.

9.

Teria tua forma – se
fosse possível esculpir
a geometria do vento; os rumores

ancestrais timbrados em teu lábio.

Edificar-te com palavras – lançar
ao vazio tuas linhas cubistas
ao ponto
        de perder-te (quase)

à bordo do impasse – é
trabalho de ourives
sem o ouro. Inda

que a noite cromática declame
o teu enigma,

a face do tesouro
se desmancha.

9.

It would have your form—if
it were possible to sculpt
the geometry of the wind; ancestral

murmurings engraved on your lips.

With words to recreate you—to cast
into space your cubist lines
to the point
          of (nearly) losing you

aboard impossibility—is
the work of goldsmiths
without gold. Even though

chromatic night proclaims
your mystery,

the treasure's face
falls apart.

10.

Canto e tua ausência soa
como um gatilho. Incende
o espectro
              das palavras
por onde passo.

Amor
é o que nasce
              para dentro. E

escoa rente
à senha do teu nome.

onde amanheço
há um mar de náufragos
e uma noite que cintila. As

horas caem
e são pétalas de fogo
no meu sono.

Canto e um rumor
de asa insone rompe
o olvido.

Para onde derrapa esse vôo?

10.

I sing and your absence echoes
like a trigger. The ghost
of words
         through which I pass
bursts into flame.

Love
is what is born
           within. And

it trickles away
at the password of your name.

Where I dawn
there is a sea of castaways
and a night that sparkles. The

hours fall,
petals of fire
in my sleep.

I sing and the rustle
of a sleepless wing penetrates
oblivion.

Where is that flight dropping to?

MAR SEM ONDAS

Cedo, ca tal a quis[o] Deus fazer
que, se a non vir, non posso viver.

D. Dinis

SEA WITHOUT WAVES

Quickly here, since God has willed it so,
that if I do not see her, I cannot live.

D. Dinis

1.

Ao retornar à memória
das asas
       para alcançar
o que fecunda a lírica (sob
estilhas de luas
imutáveis) canto
ao coração fendido
e ermo. Canto
ao silêncio ancestral
no que se exaure
e cintila. Ali
na dimensão da farpa
intrínseca, no
limiar do álibi, onde
o amor constrói seu layout,
sua lava de sangue
e rubis.

1.

Returning to the memory
of wings
        to reach
what makes the lyric fertile (beneath
splinters of immutable
moons) I sing
to the sundered
solitary heart. I sing
to ancestral silence
in which one is exhausted
and one glitters. There
in the dimension of the intrinsic
barb, on
the threshold of the alibi, where
love constructs its layout,
its lava of blood
and rubies.

2.

(...) e a que mãos dedico
estas pupilas ávidas?

Para quem sibila
essa vertigem súplice?

Tudo se alista ao súbito
fluir de adeuses, ao lapso
impreciso de sabre
cortando chuva; tudo
rinha.
        Tudo runa: pedra

de encantaria.

E mesmo os vocábulos
insurretos
            diluem-se
nos dias imperfeitos.

2.

… and to what hands do I dedicate
these avid eyes?

For whom this whisper
of suppliant dizziness?

Everything enlists in a sudden
flow of farewells, in the imprecise
instant of a saber
cutting rain; everything
a petty ruin.
            Everything a rune: stone

of enchantment.

And even insurrecting
words
        dissolve
in these
imperfect days.

3.

Segue, em anexo, ao lago
(de espelhos) íntimo
este sol que respira
facas, que assola
dentro, carnívoro
como um beijo.

Daí esta rama de sangue
na voz.

(Ó temores que assaltam
minha pequena súplica!)

Acordo para os dias
onde o sol de metal
me rasura; e aceito
que as palavras me sujem
do mundo (e cinjam
à essência o que fora
inocência).

No hoje (que é remoto)
nenhum caminho
                            está pronto.

3.

By attachment, there will follow, to the
intimate lake (of mirrors)
this sun that breathes
stilettos, that lays waste
within, carnivorous
as a kiss.

Therefore this branch of blood
in my voice.

(Oh the fears that attack
my little supplication!)

I awake to days
in which a metal sun
erases me and I allow
words to soil me
with the world (and bind
to my essence what once was
innocence).

In this today (far off already)
no path is
          ever finished.

4.

Aos pequenos apelos deste
sol de âmbar – que
o olho irisa à revelia
de cimitarras e cicuta – arde

uma cidade sob as veias.

– Raia o amor em seu monolito.

E um comboio de asas
negras dança à
(insidiosa) cesura das palavras.

Juntam-se aos lanhos
                    as algaravias
em que vicejam glicínias
incendiadas. Junta-se

ao silêncio insone o som
em que se erguem
as vigas do poema.

4.

Beneath the small appeals of this
amber sun—that
the eye makes iridescent, ignoring
scimitars and hemlock—a city

burns within my veins.

—Love radiates in its monolith.

And a convoy of black
wings dances
the insidious caesura of words.

The scribblings in which
                              wisteria
flourish in flames
merge with my lashings. The sound

with which the rafters of the poem
are lifted high
merge with sleepless silence.

5.

Sonhos famintos avançam
no poema em curso. São
tigres incendidos de relâmpagos;
fantasmas com molares
de brilhantes: senhas
que o amor instala em nossa
fibra ótica; são lã/nhuras
lúdicas, luares encravados
na sintaxe, em que o
poema, içado à superfície
das palavras, vai
escorrendo a alma às golfadas.

5.

Starving dreams move forward
in the poem in progress. They are
tigers ablaze with lightning;
ghosts with molars
made of diamonds: signs
that love erects in our
optic fibers; they are playful
catspaws, moonlight nailed
to syntax, in which the
poem, hoisted to the surface
of words, gushes out its soul in spasms.

6.

O inverno que desola
os nervos (no longo
refrão da espera) inverna
o ser: o inverno que
inverna a seco, a inundar
o ciclo das coisas findas,
acessa o mar sem
onda ao coração.
Aos poucos o amor
atraca as velas
onde a dor constrói
seu condomínio.

6.

Winter that leaves our
nerves desolate (in the long
refrain of waiting) turns being
wintry: winter that
turns wintry dry, drowning
the cycle of things that perish,
joining the sea without waves
to the heart.
Bit by bit love
furls its sails
where suffering constructs
its condominium.

7.

De tudo resta
o que se pode escoimar
ao deserto e à sua
inaudível litania.

Sob esse fio
               de lâmina
os sonhos
               fraturados
se desossam.

(Que vôo transvaza
o indizível? Que
dístico ou
sanha dos deuses?)

Apenas
uma raga esplende
a corda dos nervos.

Sob o chão dos rastros
o jogo está posto.

E uma noite implacável
turva as pedras do xadrez.

7.

Of it all what remains is
what can be sifted
from the desert and its
inaudible litany.

Below the whetted
                        blade
lie broken
            dreams
deboned.

(What flight pierces
the inexpressible? What
couplet or
what fury of the gods?)

Only
a raga can give splendor
to the chord of nerves.

Beneath a trail of prints
the game is set.

An implacable night
obscures the pieces on the board.

8.

Noite é este fruto
que foge para a casca;

esta luz recuada
ao esquecimento.

Quando as palavras
adoecem,
é da noite que elas
sangram, farpadas
em sua musculatura.

Dá para assistir
ao coração solfejar
ante a premissa
do amor. Dá
para ouvir cantar
os ossos.

... e esta noite incisa
na memória
como uma cicatriz.

8.

Night is the fruit
that flees into its shell;

this light withdrawn
into forgetfulness.

When words
grow ill,
they bleed with night,
barbed in
its muscled mass.

One can attend
the singing scales of the heart
as it faces the premises
of love. One can
hear the bones
as they sing.

... and this night chiseled
into memory
like a scar.

9.

Com o faro afeito ao vinho
e ao torpor
            de almíscar, eis
o louco em seu abrigo; esse
que finge
            cerzir abismos, esse
que em sua lã de fogo
edita Eros: eis
o faquir em seus desacatos.

Também a vã escória
tem sua lira,
sob o mais transitório
um deus conspira
a bailar sobre paixões
e cactos.

9.

Like a nose accustomed to wine
and the torpor
             of musk, behold
the madman in his shelter; the one
who pretends
             to sew shut the abyss, the one
who in his cloak of flame
edits Eros: behold
the fakir in his insolence.

Decadence, as well,
must have its lyre;
beneath the things most transitory
a god conspires,
dancing upon passions
and cactuses.

10.

Se se pudesse cardar
as estações (escandi-las como
se versos fossem) no tempo,
para encontrar o desejado (e
não vivido), essa porção
do ontem des/havida;

se se pudesse, então, voltar
a fita, rever o *making off*,
essa porção do haver-se anverso
do que se ganha sem se desejar
na vida que se doa por perder-se.

10.

If one could disentangle
the seasons (scanning them like
verses) from time,
to find the yearned for (and
not the lived), that piece
of yesterday that was and wasn't;

if one could, then, turn
back the film, watch again the outtakes,
those pieces of happening in reverse,
from which one gains without desire
in a life one gives while losing it.

MAR DERIVA

"Se não tivesse voz
A garça seria apenas
Um montinho de neve."

Sôkan

SEA DRIFT

If it had no voice
The heron would be nothing
But a mound of snow.

Sôkan

I. – Raio

Para Simone

Então seguiremos a cítara
que açoita as palavras
ou
    essa faia
que aturde o olho
dos videntes?

Como conter o mar
que transborda a sal
e a cicuta

E que tange
aos amantes a centelha
que frutifica?

Ó mantra secreto do desejo!

Passo a passo
- entre penhascos -
o coração demite seus rivais.

(E em nós
uma semente rasga o muro.)

Temos pressa
de regressar ao futuro.

I. — *Lightning*

For Simone

Then will we follow the zither
that whips words
or
    that fissure
that bewilders the gaze
of fortunetellers?

How to contain the sea
that overflows salt
and hemlock

and that lashes
towards lovers the spark
that will bear fruit?

Oh secret mantra of desire!

Step by step
—between towering cliffs—
the heart dismisses its rivals.

(And in us
A seed slowly rends the wall.)

We rush
to return to the future.

II.

(...) e no entanto estamos todos possuídos
do indizível. Imantados
por essa névoa pétrea
onde os sonhos guardam
seus víveres.

Sem relevo,
os dias se revezam
em sua fome de avessos.

Ó abrigo das coisas simples
que açula em nós
a tormentosa febre
das águas!

Ó sanha que adoece a cura!

Voláteis, somos a libélula
que no vôo se evola.

E no entanto algo de pedra
esculpe o efêmero.

Um raio de sol
devassa o lugar do nunca.

II.

… and nonetheless we are all possessed
by the inexpressible. Magnetized
by that stony fog
in which dreams store
their provender.

Without relief
days replace each other
in their hunger for the other side.

Oh refuge of simple things
that provokes in us
the tempestuous fever
of the waters!

Oh rage that turns cure to malady!

Winged creatures, we are the dragonfly
that as it flies evolves.

And nonetheless something of stone
is sculpting the ephemeral.

A beam of sunlight
penetrates the place of never.

III.

Amanheço para dentro
das palavras, tua república
de lábios,
teu éden de cicuta;

(Ó jardim de estrogênio!)

desato o verbo em que traslada
minha ereção de argila (para
além do espelho de luas
em que se nascemorre);

rabisco o coração no muro,
rasgo a tertúlia
em que o amor
navalha sob pétalas.

O que nos salva
(por pouco) nos envenena:
o visgo que vai
da carne ao poema.

III.

I dawn within
words, your republic
of lips,
your Eden of hemlock;

(Oh garden of estrogens!)

I release the word in which
my erection of clay is carried (far
beyond the mirror of moons
in which our birthdeath lies);

I scrawl my heart on the wall,
and tear in two the gathering
in which love
slashes away beneath the petals.

What saves us
(just barely) poisons us:
the sap that goes
from the flesh to the poem.

IV.

O raro vem da borda,
esquivo, farpado de luas,
a fisgar o chão
dos olhos.

E a clave que o gesto
prenuncia
                despe
a cor que brota
da rasura. Abrem-se

as rodovias
de uma vontade feita de néctar;
                              agregam-se

ao coração-garagem
o que é sofrência (e finta) e/ou
restolhos do que se colhe
sem plantar:

são códices, vozes, ondas
que inundam meus hidrantes,

para que ao fim o abismo cante.

IV.

The rare comes from the borders,
skittish, barbed with moons,
hooking itself on the plain
of the eyes.

And the music the gesture
foreshadows
          strips bare
the color that bursts forth
from the stain. Highways

open themselves
with a willingness like nectar;
                    there gathers

at the garage-heart
all of suffering (and a feint) and/or
remains of what is harvested
though never planted:

they are codices, voices, waves
that inundate my hydrants

so that, in the end, the abyss may sing.

V.

Palavras são escudos de âmbar.
Litografias: cores
encravadas na poesia,
essa vulva exposta ao signo.

Há uma febre secreta
nas coisas que pedem
para ser ditas.

Carrego este assédio
tatuado de cicatrizes.

Palavras que oxidam na mão
dos amantes; palavras
que secam
              de abandono

como o apelo dos suicidas.

Sou viajor que perdeu
seus mares
e a terra está suja de ossos.

Ouço o tambor matinal
do coração que alimenta
os sábados
e os dias sem nome.

O amor me quer virtual
entre safiras e chacais,
e entranhado durmo
na pele desse cascalho.

V.

Words are shields of amber.
Lithographs: colors
inlaid in poetry,
that vulva exposed to its sign.

There is a secret fever
in things begging
to be spoken.

I bear that importuning
tattooed with scars.

Words that rust in the hands
of lovers; words
that wither
              from abandonment
like the cry of suicides.

I am the wanderer who has lost
his seas
and the earth is befouled with bones.

I hear the morning drum-beat
of the heart that feeds
my Saturdays
and my nameless days.

Love wishes me virtual
among sapphires and jackals,
and pierced I sleep
on this pelt of broken stone.

VI.

Caminho entre a vertigem
e o fogo impresso
na grife dos dias. Onde
eu morri de ausência,
raia (prismático) o espectro
da palavra: matilhas
de metáforas.

- A lírica vestiu minhas cidades
rotas.

Agora, quando a noite alastra,
ouço esgares da fênix
encantada sobre meus rastros;

brotam lírios da ferrugem
onde a dor desfibra
meu grito de incêndios.

O amor é essa gota vazada
de amora, e o grão
que me ergue
este lacre de sangue.

VI.

On I slog between dizziness
and the fire imprinted
on the trademark of the day. Where
I died from absence
the ghost of the word
blazes (prismatic):
packs
of metaphors.

—The lyric clothed my broken
cities.

Now, as night spreads wide,
I hear foreboding cries of
the enchanted phoenix on my trail;

lilies of rust blossom forth
where suffering shreds
my cry of flames.

Love is that drop oozing
from the berry, and the grain
that grows for me
this sealing wax of blood.

VII.

Meus olhos conhecem a nudez
das sombras
- onde a réstia do vivido
encontra sua escarpa. (Olhos
são despistes para colher
vertigens. Deles
os ritos do amor
desatam seus enxames: sangram
rubis na crosta do poema.)

Meus olhos alimentam-se
de tecer incêndios: um atear-me
                                    à fratura
a distar um outro outro.

(Ou um dar-me ao risco
em que da pupila
a vida inteira se esculpisse?)

O que faço é inundar-me
como se ao mar
o deserto se despisse.

VII.

My eyes know the nakedness
of shadows
—where the weave of what's been lived
finds its jagged slope. (Eyes,
false paths for gathering
vertigo. From them
the rites of love
release their swarms and they bleed
rubies on the crust of the poem.)

My eyes feed themselves
By weaving flames: one incites me
                                    to the fray,
another banishes me to another other.

Or could it be a leaping into danger
in which all of life
takes shape within my eyes?)

What I do is flood myself
like desert stripping bare
before the sea.

VIII.

Seria o labor de Eros
o que instaura o deserto
confrontante? Ou

a espessa ramagem de vias
ínvias ao escárnio
de um deus-
michê?

A chama enfuna o coração
saltimbanco
ante os dias ao revés
colhidos na memória.

Achar-me é o assédio
que se extrema,
                         o abrigo,
em tudo que germine
ou gema.

A vida quer sangue.

VIII.

Could it be the work of Eros
that has set the desert
there before us? Or

the thick foliage of plaited
paths to the mocking laughter
of a strumpet
god?

Flames swell the heart,
that juggler
facing days in reverse
gathered in the memory.

To find myself is the endless search
that stretches me beyond myself,

                    the refuge,

in all that germinates
and groaning grows.

Life wants blood.

IX.

Saberemos eclodir o magma
do coração escarpado
quando o sangue é o nosso
único refúgio?

Deixaremos ao desterro
essa faina (fátua) da noite
a moer a inocência?

O amor está deserto. Posso
assistir à ferrugem
das horas ante o que sonha
e o que seca;

posso perder-me entre cães
sem lua: grito desfiado
em sílabas.

O que há é o entrelace,
a litania da palavra ao tempo.

E sua têxtil agonia.

IX.

Will we know how to bring to light the magma
of the steep-sloped heart
when blood is our
only refuge?

Will we leave to the desert
that (vain) drudgery of night
gnawing innocence?

Life is a wilderness. I am able to
accompany the rusting
of the hours before what dreams
and what dries out;

I am able to lose myself among dogs
without a moon: a cry unraveling
in syllables.

What's there is an intermingling,
the litany of the word in the face of time.

And its weave of anguish.

X. Nadires

A sanha que aquece a raiz dos úmeros
enseja ao coração um disparate,
ao desvelar o que é de flor em fero,
ao se tornar fiel ao que lhe mate.
São forças que nos raptam a um sem número
de vezes e vieses e desates,
e nos reduzem, simplesmente, a uns meros
felizes perdedores desse embate;
tal que não há trégua entre o amor e o fogo,
nem no sonho que enlaça nossa íris
nessa teia de nadas e nadires
em que tudo se rende ao mesmo jogo.
Vem da palavra a sagração dos ritos:
esta relíquia de silêncio e gritos.

X. Nadirs

The burning shoulder's rage, like bubbling yeast,
attends the foolish gestures of the heart,
as it unveils the flower in the beast,
as it turns faithful to its killer's art.

There are forces that gnaw us, hour after hour,
through endless slippage without consummation;
reducing us, stripped now of all our power,
to happy losers in our confrontation;

no truce is struck between true love and flame,
not even in the dream that snares our eye
in webs of nothing where our nadirs lie,
where everything surrenders to the only game.
But from the word, blessed rituals arise:
this reliquary of silence and of cries.

MAR ABERTO

"... Amour, amour, qui tiens si haut le cri de ma naissance, ..."

Saint-John Perse

OPEN SEA

"... Amour, amour, qui tiens si haut le cri de ma naissance, ..."

Saint-John Perse

1.

Somos a pelagem perdida do outono. E a íntima
dimensão em que o abismo impõe seus olhos.
Somos esta treva branca no rastro em que as palavras
se desnudam: algo que (entredentes) reluz um clamor
silente: desenredos, desamares a rasurar manhãs
no amanhã.

O amor respira à sombra de um felino.

1.

We are the lost coat of autumn. And the intimate
dimension in which the abyss affirms its gaze.
We are that blank darkness on the trail where words
strip bare: something that (between teeth) scintillates
silent clamoring: plotless, loveless, erasing tomorrow's morning.

Love breathes in a feline shadow.

As unhas na íris

O olhar ambíguo espreita
o movimento (no vácuo)
entre as unhas e a gula.

Adentra um certo visgo
à fome transeunte – e enreda

o cerco
           a bordo

do disfarce
                que (súbito!)
                            revela

sua malha de gatuno –

olhos que afluem dísticos de luz
e lâmina sob lá em que se oculta

sua ôntica delinquência.

A fera (e sua trágica
ternura) no afã
do mito voraz e avaro
desossa o seu tesouro.

Claws in the Iris

The ambiguous gaze catches
motion (in the space)
between claws and throat.

A certain stickiness impregnates
transitory hunger—and it lays its tangled

web
    within

its mask
       that (suddenly!)
                reveals

a sharper's shimmering coat—

eyes that flow with couplets of light
and a blade beneath the fur in which it hides

its ontological delinquency.

The beast (and its tragic
tenderness) with an appetite
of voracious, avaricious myth,
debones its treasure.

2.

Sobre nós incide uma música física; um tecido
larvar de sonhos tingindo a córnea e a linfa. Na
súplica (escarnada) do outono apenas o cantar
alumbra o que não fomos

— e o que aflora da palavra-árvore desta lavoura.

2.

A physical music falls on us; a larval weave of dreams
dyeing cornea and lymph. In autumn's supplication
(stripped of flesh) only the singing
casts light on what we never were

—and what emerges from the wordtree of my husbandry.

Interfaces

Ao viajor do deserto, ao
que vê a sarça
            flamejante;

ao viandante imprevisto, ao
que escava entranhas
                às estrelas:

o cantar
a tarde entornada
aos rastros; o tanger-se
onde só a voz
               insiste

em resgatar ao desejo
sua crosta de eus.

Interfaces

To the desert traveler, to the one
who sees the flaming
                    bush;

to the unexpected wanderer, to the one
who examines innards
                    under the stars;

singing
of the afternoon spilled
in his tracks; driving himself
to where only the voice
                    persists

redeeming from desire
its crust of selves.

3.

Reina o coração (crustáceo e flor) ermo em seu
contêiner a fundir a pedra ao mar; e reina ao templo
dos espelhos: vai fiando em desalinho seu culto ao
oculto, seu mudo antimundo.

Na casca do peito (incrustado) o coração ovula
pérola.

3.

The heart reigns (crustacean and flower), solitary in its
container, sinking its stone before the sea; and it reigns in the
temple of mirrors: weaving and weaving in disarray its worship of
the hidden, its anti-world curled silent.

In the shell of the breast the heart (encrusted) ovulates
a pearl.

Nidos de pájaros idos

Por vezes são só insinuações
de incêndios, tramas,
nidos de pájaros idos
como nas jóias rituais
de Liliana Reyes O.

(Um remoto havido
editado ao tempo:
marcas de dinossauro.)

Os sonhos já não gritam
(na carne)
são sítios na memória,
como impressões rupestres;

são digressões
indistintas
            de formas
aludidas pelos pássaros.

Nidos de pájaros idos*

At times they merely intimate
conflagrations and intrigues
nidos de pájaros idos
as in the ritual jewelry
of Liliana Reyes O.**

(A remote event
catalogued in time:
the markings of a dinosaur.)

Dreams no longer cry out
(in the flesh)
they are sites in memory,
like stone-carved scripts;

indistinct
digressions
          of shapes
hinted at by birds.

---

*   "Nests of Departed Birds" in Spanish.
** Columbian plastic artist influenced by pre-Columbian art and myth.

Réstia

Talvez seja só esta
manhã
       obsessiva – este
exílio
que atravessa os olhos –
a única réstia.

E o vôo
soletrado ao mármore
ante o circo de ruínas
e a dança dos búzios.

Talvez não haja
mas que um raio,
uma centelha
          encravada,
onde um deus lambe
a memória.

Beams of Light

Maybe it is just this
obsessive
        morning—this
exile
piercing the eyes—
the only beam of light.

And the flight
spelled out on marble
in the face of circled ruins
and the dance of divining shells.

Maybe there is
nothing but a ray,
a flash
        transfixed
where a god is licking
memory.

Soletude

Pour Sarah

Teu olhar ofídico (todas
essas luas perfiladas)
          secreta
a centelha por onde
            escorrem
os olhos de Deus. Atonal

e versátil
como os códices
          da água.

De que abismo
          solar
(ou remoto mar)
se esgarça essa planura?

Do plasma hebreu
           errante
(em que luzes sob a lenda),
o hoje acolhe a memória
dos teus rastros. O hoje –

que assalta
os milênios e exorta
o inaudível
          tempo
a florir desertos –
alça
      teu brilho sobre
Paris,
sobre as tulipas
         adolescentes.

Solitude

Pour Sarah

Your serpent gaze (all
those moons aligned)
                              secretes
the spark through which
                              the eyes
of God come streaming. Atonal
and versatile
like codices
                    of water.

From what solar
                    abyss
(or distant sea)
does this prairie spread and widen?

From the plasma of the wandering
                    Jew
(where you glow beneath the legend),
the day gathers the memory
of your markings. The day—
that assaults
millennia and exhorts
inaudible
                    time
to make deserts bloom—
lifts up
          your brilliance over
Paris
and its adolescent
                    tulips.

Agarro-me à centelha
do teu ouro ofídico

em que existires é
morrer-me ao abrigo
das palavras;

habitas a fervura
que o desejo acende
no lugar dos olhos

e um viés que sonha
instala iluminuras
sob os teus pés.

Miríades de tempo atroz
a conjurar
teus exílios,

ó corça assustada
entre lavas!

o olhar em cena
lacrimalha um sol
que sangra. E
aceito essa réstia
por onde migra
tua dor remota.

Venho da terra lúbrica, venho
do raio
            que ilumina
a fronteira do silêncio;

aporto à sombra
desse acorde em
que existires
            é o abrigo da linguagem.

I cling to the spark
of your ophidian gold

where your existence
is me dying in the shadow
of my words;

you inhabit the fervor
desire enflames
instead of my eyes,

and a dreaming detour
erects illuminated letters
beneath your steps.

Myriads of excruciating time
conjuring
your disappearances

oh frightened doe
amid the lava!

The unveiled gaze
cries a mesh of sun
that bleeds. And
I accept these beams, these rays,
through which your distant
pain continues its migration.

I come from a lubricious land, I come
from the beam of light
                    that illumines
silence's frontier;

I dock in the shadow
of that chord
where your existence
                    is the refuge of my language.

Ante o horto desolado
(a um vestígio do teu gesto)
ergo esta constelação
                    errante.

E vívido estala
o amor na casca
              movediça
como um rasgo
de sol na carne.

As coisas morrem
para dentro. As coisas
morrem sem piedade. E
agarro-me
            ao teu vulto
entre cascalhos
da cidade imaginária.

Te reinvento,
e as palavras quebram
no teu gelo.

À margem da via-crúcis
ardem os dias
sem rito
        e sem promessa.

E vívido estala o amor
no rasgar sem corte,
no dar-se ao ritmo
de tua música de pétalas.

Ó fênix da saga que sangra!

Meu é apenas o princípio
sem pegadas.

Before the abandoned orchard
(a vestige of your motion)
I erect this wandering
                    constellation.

And alive love
crackles in the moving
                    shell
like sun tearing
at one's flesh.

Things die
from the outside. Things
die without pity. And
I cling
                    to your shape
amid the rubble
of an imaginary city.

I reinvent you,
and the words break
upon your ice.

Along the via-crucis
days burn
without ritual
                    and without promise.

And alive love crackles
a tearing without a cut,
a surrender to the rhythm
of the music of your petals.

Oh phoenix of the saga that bleeds!

Mine is just a beginning
no footsteps to be followed.

Quem?

Para que serve esta labuta errônea
do coração ao que jamais se doma?

Quem dá partida à trama do desejo
que se distende ao acaso e ao ensejo

de um domador que dorme com a loucura?
E quem amarra os nós dessa costura

num tecido que o próprio tempo esgarça
como se feito em linhas de fumaça?

Who?

What's the use of all this drudgery, this pain,
for something that my heart can never gain?

Who first designs the drama of desire
that swells with circumstance and chance to fire

a conqueror who sleeps a maddened dream?
Who ties the knots that seal the gaping seam

within a fabric time itself will fray,
a weave of smoke that softly steals away?

A pelagem da tigra

São feitas de crisântemos as fibras
desse fogo que se molda à palavra
(e a esse jogo em que o amor se equilibra
como se a vida, então, lhe fosse escrava);
ou, talvez, da pelagem de uma tigra
(que ocultasse um vulcão em sua lava)
para blefar que fica enquanto migra
para fingir que beija quando crava.
Mas isto são hipóteses ou arenga
ao que se queira e não está à venda:
um terçar de lábios na carne brusca.
São só pegadas do que seja a lenda
de algum tesouro que se nos ofusca,
que ao tê-lo não se tenha mais que a busca.

Tiger Fur

Chrysanthemums, the fibers of this fire
that molds itself to words, that takes their shape
(and fits the game where balanced on a wire
love sways, as if life now were just its slave);
Or maybe they are made of tiger's fur
(that hides volcanic flames behind its play)
to sink its fangs as it pretends to purr,
to go away as it pretends to stay.
But these are just hypothesis that veil
with talk what you desire that's not for sale:
A sudden clash of lips on flesh, on skin.
The tracks, no more, of some forgotten tale
of treasure that bewilders us and takes us in,
so winning it we only win chagrin.

Afterword by Antonio Cicero

Tiger Fur by Salgado Maranhão is, above all, a book of love poems, written in an extraordinarily rich, imagistic, original language. These are passionate poems, filled with violently beautiful and unexpected metaphors, in which sensuality and delicacy, dream and matter, subtlety and rage all play a part. Such poems are without doubt, to use an expression from the author himself, "scored by existence."

It isn't a question of, let us say, visceral poetry, the kind that, treating art as a direct expression of life, dispenses with the intervention of formal elaboration. On the contrary, one of the most notable characteristics of Salgado Maranhão's poetry is its reflective character, enhanced exactly by its control of the techniques of composition, by its precise use of language, in a word, by its formal refinement. This helps us understand how he was able to declare, courageously, against the flow of fashion, that "there is a wide-held view of poetry and of the arts in general that is closely related to a careless Dionysian posture, one without rigor. I have never allowed myself to be like that. I've always taken an Apollonian position." He is, without doubt, telling the truth. Nevertheless, let's reconsider a passage from that declaration: *"I have never allowed myself* to be like that." This suggests that, had he allowed himself to be like that, he would have been Dionysian. And so, it is this triumph over a natural inclination of which he is, quite rightly, proud. That the Dionysian would have been a natural inclination for him is confirmed by the vital exuberance of his verses. That Apollo has the last word, however, is proven, on the one, hand by the fact that his exuberance reveals itself in a figurative and phanopaico manner and, on the other, by the obvious rhythmic control of his language.

In any case, probably the most remarkable characteristic of the poems in *Tiger Fur*, their "secret," is their capacity to foster a co-joining and interpenetration of the opposites of which they are constructed, in such a way that, instead of either one of the two losing or dulling its extreme character, each grow more accentuated.

I will take as an example of this the first poem in the book. We see right away that it is an impassioned poem: *O amor editou suas garras / em meu delírio (Love left its claws engraved / in my delirium)* are the first two lines. Before them, however, the very title of the poem "Pré-logos," cannot fail to make us think. By using that expression, where one would have expected simply "Prologue," Salgado Maranhão does not merely make the etymology of these words manifest through the change of the Greek prefix *pro* to the Latin *pre*, hyphenated, while returning to the Greek *logos*, but suggests something much more important. And that is the poet's aspiration to make his poem reach what can be found beyond/behind the *logos*, a word which, in the present context, signifies reason or language already articulated in accord with a predetermined understanding or common sense. In truth, he is trying to make the word reveal what is found *submerso como o pulsar / das pedras (submerged like the pulsing / within stones)*. Without doubt, then, he is yearning for something impossible; but—here I will quote from Paulo Ronai—"isn't the object of all art something impossible?"

In this same poem, one reads: *Por isso grito / para que as palavras / me reconheçam. (That's why I scream / so the words / will know me.)* The scream is the inarticulate, what is not yet known, and springs from a throat that itself is still inarticulate and unknown. At the same time, the scream and the throat, paradoxically, are identified with silence, in opposition to everything that is already encountered articulated in accord with common understanding, that is to say, in opposition to all that is assumed to be known and recognized, both in the world and in our selves. But, for the poet, such pretentious understandings, familiarities and recognitions are no more than worn-out words, whose effect is precisely that of preventing silence, the scream, the throat, the real, from reaching us.

In the face of all this, the poet finds himself, at first glance, at a dead end. If, on the one hand, worn out words block access to the real, on the other, the inarticulate does not manage to become the knowledge or recognition of anything at all. But the poet does not place things in such a static opposition. Let us listen to him once again: *Por isso grito / para que as palavras / me reconheçam (That's why I scream / so the words / will know me.)* This time we hear the scream as something entirely different from silence. In fact, quite the contrary, it is now an appeal of the poet to words, that they may comfort him, listen to him, recognize him. One of the meanings of this call, this appeal to words, is—forgive my abuse of the word—the recognition by the poet that he is not in total control of them. In fact, it is the worn out words that produce the illusion that words are simply the docile instruments of the one who uses them. One must, in fact, abandon this illusion, and respect their character as things partially opaque, scratched, and possessed of a specific materiality, of their own irreducible consistency. The call, the appeal, consists of a dynamic relationship in which the inarticulate (the scream) turns toward the articulate (words). The desired recognition consists in the inverse relation, in which the articulate turns to face the inarticulate. The poem does not arise from one side or the other, but from a kind of compromise of the two, a mediation, through the poet's work, both intuitive and artistic, with the specific matter of language: for the poet, that is, with his hands in the dough, producing, as Salgado Maranhão says, "a twisted music," in which, strangely enough, as in "Pré-logos," there is an articulation of interwoven opposites: the inarticulate and the articulate, the Dionysian and the Apollonian, the erotic and reflective, and so forth. Such are the poems in this book.

Alexis Levitin's thirty-six books of translation include Clarice Lispector's *Soulstorm* and Eugenio de Andrade's *Forbidden Words*, both from New Directions. Recent books include Salgado Maranhão's *Blood of the Sun* (Milkweed Editions, 2012), Eugenio de Andrade's *The Art of Patience* (Red Dragonfly Press, 2013), Ana Minga's *Tobacco Dogs* (The Bitter Oleander Press, 2013) and Santiago Vizcaino's *Destruction in the Afternoon* (Diálogos Books, 2015). Forthcoming books include Sophia de Mello Breyner Andresen's *Exemplary Tales* (Tagus Press, 2015) and Rosa Alice Branco's *Cattle of the Lord* (Milkweed Editions, 2016). In 2012, Levitin and Maranhão completed a three-month reading tour of the USA with *Blood of the Sun*, visiting over fifty colleges and other institutions.

Salgado Maranhão won the prestigious Prêmio Jabuti in 1999 with *Mural of Winds*. In 2011, *The Color of the Word* won the Brazilian Academy of Letters highest poetry award. Most recently, the Brazilian PEN Club chose his new collection, *Mapping the Tribe,* as best book of poetry for the year 2014. His newest book is *Opera of Nos*, launching in June in Rio de Janeiro. In addition to ten books of poetry, he has written song lyrics and made recordings with some of Brazil's leading jazz and pop musicians. His work has appeared in numerous magazines in the USA, including *Bitter Oleander, BOMB, Cream City Review, Dirty Goat, Florida Review, Massachusetts Review,* and *Spoon River Poetry Review*. This past summer he completed a collaboration with Alexis Levitin on the translation of *Opera of Nos*.